Disney · PIXAR

MONSTERS UNIVERSITY

Level 2

Re-told by: Marie Crook
Series Editor: Rachel Wilson

Before You Read

In This Book

Mike   Sulley   Dean Hardscrabble

Activity

Look at the pictures.
What can you see?

Mike is a monster. He goes to Monsters
University. Mike wants to be scary.

Mike meets Sulley.

Sulley does *not* work hard, but he is scary.

Mike works hard, but he is *not* scary.

Mike and Sulley are in the School of Scaring. Their teacher is Dean Hardscrabble. She is very scary!

Mike and Sulley are not friends. They fight.
They break Dean Hardscrabble's Scream Can!
Whoops! She's very angry.

Mike and Sulley are sorry. But Dean Hardscrabble tells them to leave the school. This is bad! They want to stay.

Mike has an idea—the Scare Games!
Dean Hardscrabble says they can win the
games and stay at school … or lose and leave!

Mike and Sulley find a team—Oozma Kappa.
They are not scary!
Mike thinks it's time to work!

Oozma Kappa play the games. They try hard! Their team isn't strong or fast. But they work together.

They lose some games,
but they win one game!
And Mike and Sulley
are friends now.

Then Dean Hardscrabble asks Sulley, "Do you think Mike is scary?"

Sulley has an idea! He can make the games *easy* for Mike.

Mike wins for Oozma Kappa!
But Sulley cheats. Then Mike sees it!
Suddenly, he understands. Sulley doesn't think
Mike is scary.

Mike is sad. "I *am* scary," he thinks.
I can scare a child … *ROOOAAR!*
The child isn't scared. She smiles!

Now Mike knows it's true. He's not scary.
Sulley finds Mike. He says sorry about the
Scare Games.

The friends leave Monsters University.
They get jobs!
Mike isn't scary but he's a good friend.

After You Read

1 **Read and say Yes or No.**

    1 Sulley works hard at Monsters University.

    2 Oozma Kappa win the Scare Games.

    3 Dean Hardscrabble thinks Mike is scary.

    4 Sulley makes the Scare Games easy for Mike.

2 **Choose the right word.**

> break   cheats   leave   scary   Sulley   wants

    1 Dean Hardscrabble is very ....

    2 Mike .... to be scary

    3 .... is a big blue monster.

    4 Mike and Sulley .... Dean Hardscrabble's scream can.

    5 Sulley .... in the Scare Games.

    6 Mike and Sulley .... Monsters University.

Picture Dictionary

break

lose

fight

monsters

scare / scary

team

together

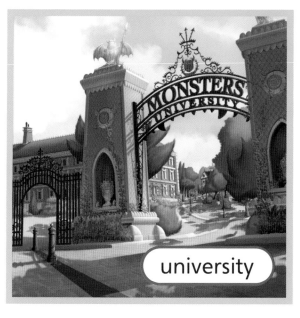

university

win

Phonics

Say the sounds. Read the words.

V v

arrive

leave

th

this

that

Say the rhyme.

At this university,
A monster team is there.
They arrive and they leave,
And they make the children scared!

Values

Work together.

Our team is bad. We can't win the games.

Yes, we can!

Then the team works together ...

We're winning the games!

We're a great team!

Find Out

How do you play these team games?

Soccer, basketball, and baseball are team games.
In soccer, you kick the ball and run fast.
In basketball, you throw and catch the ball.
In baseball, you hit and catch the ball.
In all team games, you play together.
Then you can win the game!

soccer

basketball

baseball

Kick the ball!

Pearson Education Limited
KAO Two
KAO Park, Harlow,
Essex, CM17 9NA, England
and Associated Companies throughout the world.

ISBN: 978-1-2923-4672-4

This edition first published by Pearson Education Ltd 2020

7 9 10 8 6

Set in Heinemann Roman Special, 19pt/28pt
Printed in Slovakia by Neografia

Published by Pearson Education Limited

Acknowledgments
123RF.com: Cathy Yeulet 17, dolgachov 16, 18
Getty Images: AndrewJShearer/ iStock 18, JohnnyGreig/ E+ 21, Mike Kemp 21, Morsa Images/ E+ 21, skynesher/ E+ 20

For a complete list of the titles available in the Pearson English Readers series, visit www.pearsonenglishreaders.com.

Alternatively, write to your local Pearson Education office or to Pearson English Readers Marketing Department, Pearson Education, KAO Two, KAO Park, Harlow, Essex, CM17 9NA